Words from a mother in mourning
How to protect your child from drugs
By
Phyllis M. Babrove
Licensed Clinical Social Worker

Copyright @ 2021 (Phyllis M. Babrove)
All rights Reserved

Book cover designed by Chris Holmes

"When he shall die,
Take him and cut him out in little stars,
And he will make the face of heaven so fine
That all the world will be in love with night
And pay no worship to the garish sun."
                William Shakespeare

Dedication
This book is dedicated to my daughter, Sara Babrove—
her star forever shines

Introduction

On February 28, 2020, I lost my forty-seven-year-old daughter for the final time. Final, because there had been many times (too many to remember) in thirty five years that she had been "lost" to us. Unknown to her family, Sara found her way into the dark world of drugs when she was twelve, with the problem intensifying throughout the years. What started out as smoking cigarettes ended up with overdosing on heroin when she was forty-three. That's when she decided to go into a drug rehab and change her life.

When Sara started to exhibit behavior problems at the age of twelve, I hadn't yet gone to school and learned what the behaviors might indicate. I took her to a psychologist, but little did I know that she needed more than what he was able to provide for her. When I received a call one day from his office staff informing me that the insurance would no longer pay for sessions because we had missed too many appointments, I didn't understand because I had only cancelled a few times. Sara confessed many years later that we would drop her off and she wouldn't go to the office. (After all these years, I still think that he should have called me about Sara not being in the sessions.) In high school there would be a robot call every day at six o'clock alerting me about Sara not being in school. Sara was the one who answered the phone and told me it was a wrong number. When I caught her skipping school, she of course denied it. I was naive and always believed what she told me.

This book is meant to provide a guide for parents about how to recognize the signs that their child may be using drugs. As a Licensed Clinical Social Worker, I have worked with many children whose behavior can lead to drug use when they are older. By dealing with the behaviors when the child is young, the parent may be able to provide appropriate interventions that will help their child take a different path. Not only is there more known about addiction today then there was when Sara was a child, there are more resources available to help combat the disease that destroys our loved ones.

Sir Francis Bacon said in 1597 that "knowledge is power." My hope is to provide information and resources to you that will give you the knowledge to save your child from taking the path that ultimately took my daughter's life. I hope that my words can help keep children and their families from dealing with the heartache that my family and I will suffer from for the rest of our days.

Phyllis M. Babrove

PART ONE

The Downfall of the American Family

"Drugs take away the dream from every child's heart and replace it with a nightmare, and it's time we in America stand up and replace those dreams." Nancy Reagan, 1986

<u>The Beginning</u>

"Drug abuse is defined as a chronic, relapsing disorder characterized by compulsive drug seeking, continued use despite harmful consequences, and long-lasting changes in the brain. It is considered both a complex brain disorder and a mental illness. Addiction is the most severe form of a full spectrum of substance use disorders, and is a medical illness caused by repeated misuse of a substance or substances." (National Institute on Drug Abuse)

The first national drug law, "The Pure Food and Drug Act," was passed in 1906. The law required ingredients to be listed on labels of patent medicines. In 1914, "The Harrison Narcotics Act" initiated the systems of medicines being prescribed by physicians. The scheduling of chemical substances was enacted and is still in use today. Under the act, opium and cocaine were outlawed for non-medicinal use. In 1937 marijuana was determined to be a controlled substance under "The Marijuana Tax Act." By 1971, President Nixon stated that drugs had become a national emergency, "afflicting both the body and soul of America." The DEA, Drug Enforcement Administration, was created to combat the drug problem.

In the 1970s, one out of nine Americans used drugs on a regular basis, with cocaine making a reappearance. With the increased use during that decade, a war against drugs was declared in the United States. The war on drugs was expanded under President Ronald Reagan. Nancy Reagan introduced the "Just Say No" program on September 14, 1986.

The Controlled Substance Act, passed in 1970, was enacted to regulate the controlled drugs. Drugs were categorized into five schedules according to their use and safety.

Schedule one drugs are those that are not used for medical purposes and have a high potential to be abused. Examples of schedule one drugs are heroin, LSD, marijuana, and ecstasy.

Schedule two drugs, considered to be dangerous, may lead to severe psychological and/or physical dependence. Some of the drugs included in this category are Vicodin, cocaine, Demerol, Oxycodone, fentanyl, and Ritalin.

Schedule three drugs have a moderate to low risk of causing physical and psychological dependence. An example is Tylenol with codeine.

Schedule four drugs have a low risk for abuse and dependence. Examples in this schedule are Darvon and Valium.

Schedule five drugs have a lower risk of abuse than the schedule four due to containing a limited number of narcotics. Examples are anti-diarrheal and cough medications.

In 2018, Congress passed the Substance Use Disorder Prevention that Promotes Opioid Recovery and Treatment (SUPPORT) to fight the opioid crisis that killed almost 47,000 Americans in the United States in 2018. The bill authorizes more funding for continuing education for medical personnel, funding to improve the prescription drug monitoring programs in the states, and money for research to find pain therapies that will replace opioids.

The Basics of Addiction

Addiction is defined as compulsive drug-seeking behavior in which the using of drugs becomes the center of a person's life when they abuse drugs. "Nearly seventy percent of those who try an illicit drug before the age of thirteen develop a substance abuse disorder in the next seven years."

Physical dependence on drugs is the change that takes

place in the body because of the frequent use of drugs, causing the body to require an increase in the amount of the drug. Psychological dependence, on the other hand, refers to the user's perception that he/she needs to have the drug. The psychological dependence has a longer-lasting effect on the person than the physical dependence.

Characteristics of addictive behavior include using a substance longer than was intended; not being able to cut down use; craving the substance; use of the drug interferes with work, school, and daily life; putting oneself in risky situations; if tolerance of the drug becomes an issue; and if there are symptoms of withdrawal when the amount is lessened.

Among the myths of drug addiction are the following:
1) A person who is addicted to drugs wants to be helped. However, the fact is one out of ten people who have a problem with alcohol, only believes he/she needs treatment.
2) Prior to being able to get better, a person addicted to drugs must hit rock bottom. The fact is that people seek help when they are fearful of losing something. A person has nothing to lose when they are at their rock bottom.
3) People who are addicted to drugs will quit without help. The fact is that most people on drugs will die without intervention.
4) Being addicted to illegal drugs is a lifestyle choice. The fact is that when drugs take over a person's life, they have no control over the cravings.
5) If someone tries to help the person who is addicted, the situation may become worse. The truth is that damages caused by the drugs may make it impossible for the person to make appropriate decisions. But an intervention by friends or family members may help the person addicted make the right choices in life.

Various risk factors influence the potential for a person to become addicted to drugs. Drug use during the teenage years is detrimental because a person's brain continues to develop into their twenties. Ninety percent of people who abuse substances started using drugs when they were teenagers. Other risk factors include having a history of family substance abuse, mental health issues, behavior problems, history of trauma in childhood, addiction in the family or among peers, access to nicotine or other substances, and the age when first used.

<u>The Enemies</u>

The five classes of drugs are narcotics, stimulants, depressants, steroids, and hallucinogens. Drugs within each class have similar effects and all are controlled substances. Except for anabolic steroids, controlled substances are used to change the mood, thinking, and emotions because of their effect on the brain and spinal cord.

Narcotics, also known as opioids, are derived from opium. Examples are heroin, oxycodone, hydrocodone, codeine, morphine, methadone, and fentanyl. Opioids create both physical and psychological dependence. They come in various forms, such as tablets, capsules, lollipops, skin patches, liquid, suppositories, powder, and syrups. Opioids are injected, swallowed, smoked, or sniffed. Teenagers can easily obtain narcotics from friends, family, medicine cabinets, and over the internet.

Heroin, processed from morphine (poppy plants) is a white or brown powder. Highly addictive, it presents a high risk for overdosing and may contain ingredients that the user is not aware of. It is common practice for heroin to be cut with other drugs, sugar, starch, powdered milk, or quinine. Pure heroin is snorted or smoked, and because it enters the brain quickly, it is extremely addictive psychologically and physically. The user experiences a surge of euphoria known as a "rush" followed by a twilight state of sleep. Heroin has a high rate of death due to the user not knowing if the drug has been cut with another substance. Signs of overdose from heroin are slow, shallow breathing; blue lips and fingernails; clammy skin; convulsions; coma; and possible death.

Oxycodone is semi-synthetic and is marketed as oxycontin. It is in the form of a tablet that is crushed and sniffed, or dissolved in water and injected. It is also heated on a piece of aluminum foil so that the vapors can be inhaled. Signs of overdose can be extreme fatigue, muscle weakness, confusion, cold and clammy skin, shallow breathing, slow heart rate, pupils that look like pinpoints, coma, fainting, and possible death.

Hydrocodon is a semi-synthetic opioid that is combined with acetaminophen (brand name is Tylenol) and is used for pain. Although it is moderately potent, if used long-term, hydrocodone may cause physical or mental dependence.

Codeine is a narcotic used for mild to moderate pain management. Long term use may be habit forming.

Morphine is non-synthetic, taken orally or injected; causes feeling of euphoria.

Methadone is synthetic in tablet or liquid form; causes psychological dependence and similar effects of morphine and heroin.

Fentanyl is one hundred times more potent than morphine, fifty times more potent than heroin. It causes relaxation, euphoria, pain relief, sedation, confusion, dizziness, nausea, vomiting, urinary retention, and respiratory depression leading to death.

Stimulants speed up the body's systems. They include amphetamines, such as Adderall, cocaine, and bath salts.

Depressants are used for reducing anxiety, inducing sleep, and preventing seizures. They afre also abused to gain a sense of euphoria and are also added to other drugs to make the "high" last longer to help curb side effects. Depressants can cause amnesia, impair judgment, and cause confusion. Most are controlled substances in the United States.

Different types of depressants include barbiturates (they depress the central nervous system); benzodiazepines (produce sedation, relieve anxiety, and stop muscle spasms); and as an anti-seizure medication.

Hallucinogens are found in plants and fungi or are synthetically produced. They alter perception and mood.

MDMN/Ecstasy tablets are made in a variety of colors. It is both a stimulant and a psychedelic drug. The tablets have logos and come in capsules, powder, and liquid.

LSD is saturated on paper with graphic designs. The majority of those who use LSD are in middle and high school.

LSD is used orally or smoked. Psychic effects are distortions of thoughts, causing flashbacks that may occur during times of stress, more often with younger users.

Anabolic Steroids are synthetic and contain testosterone to improve physical appearance, muscle growth, and athletic performance. The drug is smuggled illegally into the United States. It is used orally, injected, or applied to the skin.

According to the Center for Disease Control (CDC), the number of deaths from drug over-doses in America climbed from 16,849 in 1999 to 70,237 in 2017, with the total number in the eighteen years being over 770,000.

The results of The National Survey on Drug Use and Health conducted by the SAMHSA in 2018 revealed that 164.8 million Americans aged twelve and over had used drugs during the previous month. The substances used included tobacco, alcohol, and illicit drugs. In 2018, one out of five people aged twelve and over reported using an illicit substance during the previous year.

In 2017 one of every three children in the United States entered foster care because of parental substance abuse, an increase of fifty-three percent since 2007. According to the American Medical Association' s state report (7/20/2020), "More than thirty-five states have reported increases in opioid-related mortality as well as ongoing concerns for those with a mental illness or substance use disorder in counties and other areas within the state.

In monitoring over 42,500 students in four hundred schools in the United States in 2019, (grades eight, ten, and twelve), it was found that the drug use was lower than in the previous five years, except for marijuana use. Although the abuse of opioids was lower than at any time since the survey began, the use of vaping had continued to rise.

"In 2018, the U.S. Surgeon General called vaping an 'epidemic', and the FDA has continued to impose restrictions on manufacturers, including suspending the manufacture and sale of sweet, candy-like flavors for 'closed pod' e-cigarettes like Juul in February 2020."

Vaping was promoted as a way for people to quit smoking cigarettes. However, the FDA has not approved vaping to quit smoking. Since there aren't any guidelines on how to treat an addiction to vaping, it's an increasing concern that so many teens are becoming addicted and are not able to get the help they need.

PART TWO

Behavior, Prevention and Intervention

"Somewhere in the person's development, often in the early or formative years of life, something happens that causes a distorted self-concept." Dr. Abraham Twerski

<u>Behavior Problems</u>

Early recognition of behavior problems in children is essential to providing appropriate interventions. Research has shown that impulsive behaviors in children are indictors of substance abuse when the child becomes a teenager or young adult. According to the DSM-5 (Diagnostic and Statistical Manual of Mental Disorders, Fifth Edition) the behaviors are categorized as Disruptive, Impulse-Control, and Conduct Disorder.

Oppositional Defiance Disorder (ODD) is characterized by angry outbursts, irritable moods, defiance, and vindictive behaviors. To receive a diagnosis of ODD, at least four of the following behaviors must be present for a minimum of six months:

1. Inability to control temper.
2. Frequent exhibition of angry and resentful behaviors.
3. Becomes annoyed easily and displays overly sensitive emotions.
4. Argues with authority figures.
5. Defiant against rules.
6. Annoys and irritates other people.
7. Refuses to take responsibility for own actions.
8. Displays spiteful or vindictive behaviors a minimum of twice in six months.

"According to the American Academy of Child and Adolescent Psychiatry, if a child has a diagnosis of ODD there is a more than 90 percent chance that he will be diagnosed with another mental illness later in life. ODD also increases the risk of suicide or substance abuse. With treatment at an early age, the individual has a better chance of preventing a diagnosis of conduct disorder, becoming an addict, or engaging in delinquent behaviors."

Intermittent Explosive Disorder is the failure to be able to stop aggressive impulses. As a result, the child assaults others, destroys property, or has frequent temper tantrums. The disorder usually begins in later childhood or adolescence. Depression, anxiety, and substance abuse may follow in later years. The majority of those diagnosed with Intermittent Explosive disorder are male. To receive a diagnosis, the behaviors must occur twice a week for three months.

Conduct Disorder behaviors include repetitive behavioral and emotional problems presented by children. Unable to follow rules, children with Conduct Disorder do not respect the rights of others, show empathy, or behave in ways that are acceptable in society.

Some of the behaviors include bullying, cruelty towards people and animals, aggressive behaviors, stealing, lack of remorse, lying, and setting fires.

A pyromaniac is a person who sets fires deliberately and repeatedly. A feeling of satisfaction or release of emotions may be experienced once the fire has been lit. More males than females are pyromaniacs, and it is also more predominant in those who have learning disabilities and lack social skills.

Criteria for diagnosis of pyromania includes attraction to fire; the act of purposely setting more than one fire; a feeling of excitement or tension before the fire and pleasure or relief while it's burning; and that the purpose of the fire is not for financial gain (i.e., insurance money).

Kleptomania is the inability to resist impulses to steal

items that are not needed by the person committing the act. The person exhibits increased tension, anxiety, or arousal before the theft; a feeling of pleasure, relief, or gratification while stealing the item; and guilt or remorse after he or she has finished the act. There is then a repetition of the cycle. The items stolen are not needed but are taken due to emotional issues. The kleptomaniac resists therapy for fear of being turned over to the police.

It is important to mention two behaviors that are drawing attention for becoming addictions that may lead to substance abuse.

In 2018, the World Health Organization determined that excessive playing of video games for a minimum of twelve months can be diagnosed as an addiction. The criteria for the diagnosis are: if the gaming has a sufficient impact on the player's personal life, family participation, education, occupation, and in other vital areas of life.

Risk factors that may lead to someone with an addiction to gaming turning to substance abuse may include low self-esteem, feelings of neglect, inability to manage moods, anxiety, depression, lack of empathy or isolation. Some who are addicted to games may turn to stimulants like cocaine that will increase their drive to stay awake for longer periods of time to play the games.

Children in western countries spend an average of forty hours a week on the internet. The indicators that parents should be aware of as to whether or not their child is spending too much time on the computer are that the child loses track of time while on the computer; sleeps less to be on the computer more; becomes angry when computer time is limited; homework and chores are neglected; less time is spent with family and friends; ignores time limits that have been put in place; lies about time spent online; is moody when not on the computer; and shows less interest in activities that they once found enjoyable.

<u>Prevention</u>

Parent education is one way to help parents learn appropriate parenting techniques that can help prevent oppositional behaviors from developing. There are nine steps for parents to put in place for effective parenting:
1. Raise the child's self-esteem.
2. Praise good behavior but use praise appropriately and for good reasons.
3. Set rules and be consistent.
4. Spend quality time together.
5. Be a good role model.
6. Keep communication open.
7. Be flexible with the way parenting is conducted.
8. Show the child that love is unconditional.
9. Know limitations as a parent.

Children benefit from having structure and rules in place, along with adult supervision. Parents must be consistent with discipline and put in place a system that is appropriate for the child and the family. Resources like websites, books, and support groups are invaluable tools for all parents.

Interventions

Early interventions play a key role in preventing addictive behaviors later in life. Young children with oppositional behaviors benefit from an evaluation by a mental health professional as early as the behaviors are recognized. Behavior therapy techniques can be provided in which parents will be taught age-appropriate interventions. Oppositional behaviors can be prevented by teaching young children anger management skills and social skills.

Partnership to End Addiction provides the following guidelines for parents of pre-adolescents:
1. Make sure your child is aware of your rules regarding the use of drugs, alcohol, and nicotine.

2. Make positive comments about your child's strengths. Focus on their effort, creativity, and kindness, not on good grades or winning.
3. Know who their friends are and meet the parents.
4. Teach your child how to distinguish fantasy from reality by watching television and movies with them. It is a good teaching moment to help them learn the difference.

Prevention tips for teenagers thirteen to eighteen years old:

1. Stress the importance of rules and consequences. Be clear about your disapproval of all drugs, alcohol, nicotine, and vaping.
2. Praise your child and discuss their strengths.
3. Show interest in what they do and in their friends.
4. Build trust.

Addiction is an individual disease that is destructive to not just the person using drugs but to everyone in the substance user's circle. As the addiction increases, so does the lying and stealing. At first, we think that we misplace money or a piece of jewelry, but as it continues to happen, we try to figure out what's going on.

Information and resources are so much better today than they were when Sara was a teenager. There is more awareness of the link between early behavior problems and addiction, and more help for parents.

Teenagers are typically resistant to counseling and especially to family counseling because they like their privacy. In the case of addiction and behavior issues, the teen should receive individual therapy but also participate in therapy with the family.

PART THREE

Parenting

"It's not what you do for your children but what you have taught them to do for themselves that will make them successful human beings." Ann Landers

<u>Empowering vs Enabling</u>

Protecting our children begins the moment we learn that we are going to become a parent. We take prenatal vitamins, eat healthy foods, stop drinking alcohol and caffeine, and visit the doctor regularly. As the years go by, we teach our children right from wrong, ensure that they receive a good education, love them, and keep them safe. As parents, we do our best to make sure that they have positive influences in their life by guiding them to choose positive friends and to make the right decisions. But as all parents learn, we cannot be with them twenty-four hours a day. The time comes when we hope that they can be trusted to make decisions that will take them along the right path.

What happens when they stray from what we have instilled in them? What does a parent do when their child starts to make the wrong decisions and choose friends that have a negative influence? What do parents do when they find themselves dealing with an angry teenager or young adult, someone that they no longer recognize as their child?

As important as it is to praise and reward good behavior, it is equally important to teach a child that there will be consequences when they exhibit negative behaviors. While behavior and discipline were discussed in earlier chapters, it is important for parents to know the difference between enabling and empowering their child. The following quote by Maimonides, a medieval philosopher, illustrates the difference between the terms: "Give a man a fish and you feed him for a day. Teach a man to fish and you feed him for a lifetime."

Giving a man a fish is enabling him to not learn the skills he needs to be able to care for himself; teaching him to fish is empowering him to be independent.

In many instances, parents enable their child without realizing it. For example, Tommy's mother knows that he has been smoking marijuana with his friends. His mother is concerned not only about the marijuana use, but that he may be stealing to get money to buy it. (Tommy is fourteen and doesn't have a job). When she confronts him, Tommy responds that his friends give him the marijuana. Knowing that he wasn't being honest, she decided to have another conversation with him. Tommy finally admitted that he was using the spending money she gave him to buy the marijuana. Unknown to Tommy's mother, she had been enabling him to use marijuana by giving him money and not monitoring what he used it for.

In another scenario, Sandy (also fourteen years old) asked her parents how she could earn money so that she could buy some new skates. Her parents helped her work out a plan on how she would be able to earn money by babysitting her younger brother and sister. They also helped her figure out how long it would take her to save the money and explained the process of saving and budgeting. When Sandy had enough money saved, her mother took her shopping for the skates. Sandy's parents were involved not only in the earning of the money but also in teaching her how to save for what she wanted. In this way, they were able to empower Sandy to be responsible.

In the book, "Son Down, Son Up," Brenda Seals states, "I have learned that there are distinct, crucial differences between helping and enabling. Enabling someone makes it easier for him to continue making bad choices, exhibiting destructive behavior, and floundering in addiction."

"Are you an Enabling Parent?" is an article that was published in Psychology Today in 2016. Some of the signs of a parent who enables their child are when they are in denial that the child may be using illegal substances; not acknowledging that the problem exists because of guilt; ignoring negative behaviors; trusting the child's promises; not being consistent when giving consequences for poor behavior; forgiving the child too quickly; blaming peers for their child's behavior, and believing the lies told by their child.

The article also suggests solutions for parents who enable their children. Some of these suggestions are that both parents need to be on the same page when dealing with the child; parents should educate themselves about addiction and the process of recovery; self-care for parents; participate in a twelve-step support group, such as Ala-non, Nar-anon, or parenting support groups; parents need to support each other and realize that the road to recovery is long and difficult.

<u>Peer Pressure</u>

Merriam Webster defines peer pressure as, "A feeling that one must do the same things as other people of one's age and social group in order to be liked or respected by them."

The six kinds of peer pressure that teens face are:
1) Verbal peer pressure is when peers ask, suggest, or persuade other teens to participate in a behavior.
2) Unspoken peer pressure is how teens are pressured by the use of fashion, personal interactions, or joining a club or team. This is pressure that is generally put on younger teens by those who are older and popular.
3) Direct peer pressure is either spoken or unspoken. Examples are cheating from someone during a test or handing another teen an alcoholic drink.
4) Indirect peer pressure is done in a subtle manner such as a teen gossiping about a peer to another teen.
5) Negative peer pressure is when a peer asks a teen to do something that is against his or her moral beliefs.

6) Positive peer pressure is when a teen does well academically and is a positive influence on his or her peers.

"New research shows that, when making a decision, teens think about both the risks and rewards of their actions and behaviors—but unlike adults, teens are more likely to ignore the risk in favor of the reward."

A study conducted by the National Institute on Drug Abuse revealed that teens who were driving with friends in the car were more likely to take risks. "Results showed that just knowing friends were watching activated brain regions linked with rewards, especially when the teen drivers made risky decisions."

In the book, "Hold On to Your Kids: Why Parents Need to Matter More Than Peers," the authors state the following: "Peer-oriented kids will do anything to avoid the human feelings of aloneness/suffering, and pain, and to escape feeling hurt, exposed, alarmed, insecure, inadequate, or self-conscious. The older and more peer-oriented kids, the more drugs seem to be an inherent part of their lifestyle." They also state, "Drugs are emotional painkillers."

Some of the ways that parents cause low self-concept in children include excessive criticism, overprotecting and/or overindulging their children, neglecting their children,
expecting perfectionism and providing conditional love.

Among the ways that parents can build their child's self-concept are showing unconditional love to their child, modeling self-concept and self-care, letting the child know they are valued, and allowing the child to struggle through making decisions and owning them.

Family Support

As happens in many families when a member is addicted to drugs, there may be long periods of time when the ties are broken. This was the case in my family, but the situation changed when Sara went into a rehab program. As a social worker, I had never worked with people addicted to drugs or alcohol. As a mother, I learned a lot when Sara was in the program. Visiting was allowed on Sundays but only if the visitor attended a parenting group for an hour before the visit. The group was educational in that the members of the group were taught about the importance of supporting their family member during the recovery process.

After the group concluded, family visits were held in the cafeteria. Many of the clients, who ranged in age from eighteen into the sixties, would have visitors while others wandered around alone. Some had visits with their young children who had been brought by a family member. Sara looked forward to the visits and I looked forward to seeing her every Sunday, and to watch the progress she was making. I knew it was difficult for her and that she had a long road ahead of her. I was proud of the fact that she had decided to change her life.

The National Council on Alcoholism and Drug Dependence reports that addiction "stresses the family to the breaking point" and impacts family unity, mental and physical health, finances, and overall family dynamics. Living with addiction also puts family members under "unusual stress" and can have a dangerous impact on both adults and children as the stages of addiction progress."

Parents say that children don't come into the world with a manual or instructions and unfortunately, that is true. As our children grow, so do we as parents. From the time that they are born, we communicate with them by talking, singing, and reading stories to them. As they start speaking and walking, we teach them how to be careful and how to avoid dangerous situations. They come to us when they fall, bump into something, or are upset. We comfort them with words and soothe their feelings. And as the years go by, we still protect them from danger and talk to them about making the right decisions.

Communication between parent and child continues and strengthens throughout life. When the communication breaks down, so does the relationship. This especially becomes an issue at the beginning of adolescence when children are seeking independence and trying to find their own way. Problems may arise with peer pressure and the teen wanting to make their own decisions.

Many parents find themselves at a loss about how to set appropriate rules and boundaries when their child becomes a teenager. That's why it is important to be consistent with rules, communication, and discipline throughout the years. Children will be more open with their parents if they don't feel judged or unfairly criticized. They will know that they can talk to their parents about anything.

The Child Mind Institute suggests the followingstrategies for positive communication with teenagers: listen to what they have to say without prying; validate their feelings; show them trust by asking them to do important tasks; praise them for positive things; spend time together; and be observant as to what is going on in their life.

The Better Health Channel lists tips for positive com- munication with teenagers. They include listening to the teen more than talking to him/her, giving them privacy, being aware of the things that they are interested in, letting them know that you love them, and having fun with them while being supportive.

PART FOUR

Help Your Teen Set Goals

"I've missed more than 9,000 shots in my career. I've lost almost 300 games. Twenty-six times, I've been trusted to take the game winning shot and missed. I've failed over and over and over again in my life. And that is why I succeed." Michael Jordan

Setting Goals

As a high school social worker, I found that students who have goals are more likely to attend school regularly. They focus on being involved in sports, clubs, and achieving high grades. While some students know before they start high school what they want to do in life, I found that the majority don't. My advice to them was to think of things that they are interested in and decide what they want to pursue. It doesn't matter if goals change over the years because that's part of our growth. But having a plan helps us work to our full potential in school, at work, and in making positive decisions in life.

The main benefits of effective goal setting are to:
1. Teach adolescents to organize their time and tasks.
2. Increase their motivation and sense of achievement.
3. Teach teens about being accountable.
4. Allow adults to have a chance to be supportive of their child's interests.

Among the tips to help children set goals are to let the goal be the teen's goal, be supportive, teach them how to set the goals that will help them achieve their dreams, know the right time to talk to them about setting goals, and teach them that they are in control of their future successes.

Short-Term Goals

When I talked to students about goals, I explained that goals help us get through hurdles. Breaking down our long-term goals into short-term ones helps make them more achievable. If the plan is to go to college, it may be difficult for adolescents to "see" what they must accomplish to get there.

Examples of short-term goals may be attending school on a regular basis; doing well academically; participating in clubs and extra-curricular activities; communicating with teachers and guidance counselors; and choosing peers with similar goals and interests. Because they are short-term and attainable daily, the student can see consistent results and have a sense of accomplishment. The same strategies can be used by students who are interested in vocational school to learn trades.

<u>Long-Term Goals</u>

As teens mature, they can envision what they want to achieve over the years. Those students who are college-bound can set short-term goals to meet the requirements of getting into college. For example, they can monitor their Grade Point Average regularly, be aware of what the state graduation requirements are, what universities they want to apply to and the entrance requirements. When parents sit down with their child to help them plan for their future, it is important for the teen to be in control of their own destiny, and to know that they are supported in their choices. It not only teaches them responsibility but that the decisions they make will impact their entire life.

PART FIVE

The Reality

"As long as someone denies reality, he or she can continue behaving the same as before. Acceptance of reality might commit him or her to the very difficult process of change." Abraham J. Twerski, M.D.

<u>Life of A Person with a Drug Addiction</u>

My initial plan for this chapter was to discuss the impact that drugs have on someone's life. As I did some research, I realized that I know first-hand what they did to my child.

Sara loved school from her first day of kindergarten. Throughout the years, she would complain about teachers, and teachers would complain about her. Regardless of the minor behavior problems she had during elementary school, she did well academically. Like with many children, the behaviors escalated when she started middle school. Things started disappearing at home, causing us to think we misplaced jewelry, money, and other items. Sara became more defiant, was caught skipping school and smoking cigarettes in the park down the street; she started leaning toward the wrong kind of friends. The suspensions became more frequent, but her grades were good.

High school was more of the same—good grades and bad behaviors. She did well in her classes, won Spanish competitions, and worked at various jobs. During those years, the defiance became worse at home, school, and work. Sara was unable to maintain a job and we never knew why. Maybe she was using drugs and it caused her to be fired repeatedly? I don't know, but the pattern continued through adulthood.

After graduating from high school, Sara attended community college for a short time. One day when she was eighteen and had a boyfriend who was bringing her down even more than she already was, I gave her the choice of going out with him or living at home. (She had left three times before and I told her it was too disruptive to the rest of the family for her to leave and come back). When I came back from the grocery store, she was waiting outside with her things packed. Sara never lived with us again.

Sara had good jobs over the years and finished her education with a master's degree. With pain pill clinics located throughout the area, her addiction to opioids worsened quickly. As the addiction became more serious, the negative friends came and went, and legal problems occurred frequently. Jobs weren't kept and there were many dreadful relationships like the first one. Months would go by with no communication from her.

Over the years, I begged Sara to go to counseling or to a drug program, but she always refused, saying that she could quit on her own. In 2015, she overdosed on heroin and almost died, scaring her into going for help. She went to a detox program and then to a residential program. After three days, she left the residential, saying that she was a grown up and nobody was going to tell her what to do. Within a short time, she went back to detox and then to another residential program. When she completed the residential program, (I think it was about four months), she lived in a sober house for a short time.

Sara found a job in a telemarketing company selling health insurance. After many years of not having a driver's license because it had been revoked by the state due to legal issues, Sara was able to buy a car and rent an apartment. When sales dropped, the money stopped. She found another job but was back in the old cycle of not being able to keep it.

As time went on, things got worse for her financially. I helped her as much as I could, something I had never done before she stopped using. At the end of 2019, everything fell apart for her. She lost the apartment and was barely able to pay for her car. Working for her uncle, she was hardly able to make it on her own.

I know in my heart that Sara relapsed because she could not find a job. The more interviews she had, the less call backs she received and the more discouraged she became. She would never admit it, but Sara knew that her past mistakes had caught up with her. It broke my heart that she couldn't find what she was looking for, which was an opportunity to be able to be successful financially. Nobody would give her a chance to prove that she had changed. Sara's story is my reality, and I don't want it to become yours.

"Once the psychological or physical craving for the substance exists, it affects a person's thinking in much the same way as a bribe or other personal interest distorts one's judgment. The need for the substance is so powerful that it directs the person's thought processes to sanction or preserve the drinking or using. That is the function of addictive
thinking: to permit the person to continue the destructive habit. The more brilliant a person is, the more ingenious are his or her reasons for not being abstinent and for considering Twelve Step fellowships worthless." (Dr. Abraham Twerski)

It is estimated that between 1.9 and 2.4 million of the youth that are in the juvenile justice system have addiction issues and only 68,000 receive treatment. Statistics indicate that 44 percent of minors who are arrested for burglary have committed the crime so that they can earn money to buy drugs. One-third of teenagers that are arrested for assault are, by their own reporting, drunk or high at the time of committing the crime. "Chronic violent young offenders are three times as likely to drink alcohol and twice as likely to smoke marijuana."

Statistics show that, "Of the 22 million adults in recovery in the United States, nine percent are unemployed—that's more than double the overall rate." Some of the explanations are that the person with a substance abuse addiction has gaps between jobs that look poor on a resume and because of having criminal records.

<u>Laws</u>

In response to the opioid epidemic in the United States, the federal government passed the Substance Use Disorder Prevention that Promotes Opioid Recovery and Treatment (SUPPORT) for Patients and Communities Act of 2018. The act provides resources to train first responders on how to administer medications to prevent death during an overdose. Other provisions included in the act are recovery programs that include counseling, recovery housing, and job training.

The Comprehensive Addiction and Recovery Act authorizes one hundred and eighty-one million dollars annually to establish prevention and treatment programs to combat opioid use.

The Affordable Care Act has provisions for substance abuse treatment, as well as for mental health needs. In 2000 the federal government initiated The Children's Health Act of 2000 that provides assistance to halt the increase of amphetamine production, including drugs that are used for inhaling. The act allows drug enforcement agencies to investigate and shut down the labs as well as shut down the drug dealers.

The first drug court in the United States was established in Miami, Florida in 1989. The purpose of the program is to provide treatment to drug offenders, offering them an opportunity to stop using drugs and turn their life around. The program provides counseling, drug treatment, random drug testing and frequent appearances in court. The length of the program is from six months to one year and is monitored by the judge. There are now three thousand drug courts in the United States, half of which are targeted to adolescents and include a family counseling component.

Thirty-seven states and the District of Columbia offer involuntary commitment for those with alcohol and substance abuse addiction. To have someone committed, there must be proof that the person is addicted to alcohol or drugs. There also must be proof that the person who is being committed has attempted to hurt himself or another person or is unable to care for himself because of his addiction. If the person being committed is under eighteen years of age, a parent or guardian can force them to enter treatment.

An example of involuntary commitment is the Marchman Act in Florida. The person can be committed by someone related by blood, a spouse, or three people who are unrelated, and file a petition with the court to have the person evaluated. If the petition is accepted, there will be a court hearing to seek a court order for an evaluation. Various levels of care can be ordered for the client, depending on their individual needs. The Marchman Act is regulated by the Florida Substance Abuse Impairment Act, passed in 1993. The act provides that the person who is being involuntarily committed has certain rights that are protected. Some of these rights include that the individual always be treated with dignity, the services must meet the individual needs of the person being committed, minors are to be be provided with the education to meet their needs, client's records are guaranteed to be confidential, and the person is entitled to legal representation.

PART SIX

Effective Treatment

"To be yourself in a world that is constantly trying to make you something else is the greatest accomplishment." Ralph Waldo Emerson

<u>Path to Recovery</u>

Due to advanced technology, teenagers in today's world face different trials than in the past. With the internet, instant information is literally at their fingertips. When utilized in positive ways, going on-line is a good resource, but that's not always the case. The internet can be used for negative purposes, such as obtaining information about drugs. Social media makes it easy to connect with peers who have the same interests. Although many parents do their best to monitor the on-line activities of their child, it's not always possible.

Parents should be aware of behavioral and physical signs indicating that their child is using drugs. Among these signs are mood swings, loss of interest in activities, sudden change of friends, sleeping more than usual, breaking rules, and increased signs of anger. Other signs may be poor hygiene, avoiding eye contact, stealing, secretive calls, low grades, missing school or work, and frequently asking for money.

Research has identified thirteen "Principles of Adolescence Substance Use Disorder Treatment." They are:

1. Identify substance use as soon as possible.
2. Adolescents can benefit from some type of treatment even if they are not addicted. Substance use disorders range from problematic use to addiction, including experimenting with drugs.

3. Annual physical exams by a physician can screen for drug use.
4. Family pressure and legal interventions can be used to force the teen to get treatment.
5. It is essential that treatment meet the specific needs of the individual.
6. The treatment needs to address the whole person, including medical, psychological, and social well-being.
7. Behavioral therapies, incentives, and skills to resist drugs are vital in addressing the needs of the adolescent.
8. Keeping the family and community involved in the treatment process is essential to the adolescent's process of recovery. This is done through strengthening the family relationships and by having people in the adolescent's life who encourage treatment. These people would include peers, school staff, mentors, and others within the child's community.
9. Identifying and treating mental health disorders, along with the substance abuse disorders, will help the treatment be successful.
10. Victims of child abuse, domestic violence, or suicide within the adolescent's circle should be identified, as they often are the reasons the child turns to drug use.
11. While the adolescent is receiving treatment, it is important to monitor suspected drug use.
12. Treatment programs need to be completed as planned for them to be effective. After-care is also essential in maintaining sobriety.
13. As part of the treatment plan, adolescents should receive education for safe sex and STD prevention.

Research has shown that treatment programs lasting for a minimum of three months will be more effective for long term success. A doctor-monitored treatment plan that has medicine managed detoxification also has more positive results. Quitting drug use without medication can result in a dangerous situation, such as death. Behavioral therapy and medications help ensure a better chance of maintaining sobriety.

There are five types of programs that are designed to help adolescents with an addiction problem:
1. Early interventions that include educational information about substance abuse.
2. Outpatient treatment is approximately six hours or less per week. The time may be adjusted depending on the progress.
3. Intensive outpatient therapy is a day treatment program that the teen attends for a maximum of twenty hours per week. The length is two months to one year.
4. Residential treatment is one in which the client resides in the program twenty-four hours a day, for one month to one year.
5. If the youth's addiction is severe, a medically managed program is advised and provides medical care for twenty-four hours a day. The length depends on the teen's progress in the program.

There are several types of therapies that have shown positive results for adolescents in drug treatment programs. Cognitive Behavioral Therapy (CBT) teaches teens positive coping skills and how to be aware of problems before they develop. Teens learn how to recognize triggers that may lead them back to using drugs.

Twelve Step Facilitation Therapy is to encourage the teenager to participate in a twelve-step program that has been modified for adolescents.

Family-Based Approaches therapy addresses issues within the family system. Family conflicts, communication issues, mental health problems, learning disorders, school or work problems, and peer groups are important in the teens' progress for remaining drug-free.

Functional Family Therapy utilizes behavioral approaches to address communication, problem-solving techniques, conflict resolution, and parenting skills.

Family Behavioral Therapy addresses issues of substance abuse and other behavioral problems that the teen may be exhibiting. The therapy involves the teen, one or both parents, and the therapist. The goal of the therapy is to stop the teen from using drugs.

Programs for young adults are like those for adolescent treatment:

1. Long-term residential programs provide twenty-four-hour care and are six to eight-month programs. The programs provide comprehensive services that are targeted to the individual needs of the client.
2. Short-term residential programs are based on the twelve-step initiative and are in a hospital setting. The program, three to six weeks long, is followed by extensive outpatient care and a support program, such as Narcotics Anonymous.
3. Outpatient treatment varies in the structure of the program. In many cases, the purpose is to educate the participants about drugs. There are individual therapy sessions as well as group sessions.
4. Individual counseling deals with the client's addiction and, when present, mental health issues. The therapist will also encourage the client to participate in a twelve-step program once or twice a week.
5. Group counseling has been found to be successful for those involved with addiction.

Psychoeducational groups educate about the dangers of drugs and skills support groups teach positive coping skills. The goal of Cognitive Behavioral Therapy groups is to change learned behavior by focusing on changing the thought process. Support groups provide members with support by others who have the same concerns, and to develop their interpersonal relationship skills as they go through the process together.

Recovery is defined by the SAMHSA as "a process of change through which individuals improve their health and wellness, live a self-directed life, and strive to reach their full potential."

There are four elements of life that are essential for a person in recovery:
1. Good physical and emotional health.
2. A stable and safe home.
3. A sense of purpose that is fulfilled by having a job or going to school and being part of society.
4. Support from the community, relationships, and social groups.

The five rules of recovery are: 1) create a new life by avoiding triggers from the past that may present a high-risk situation; 2) have a support system in place that includes family, friends, counselors and attending self-help groups; 3) total honesty is required in recovery; 4) learn coping skills that will replace the drugs that were once used for coping; and 5) make a total life change in recovery in order to be successful.

Stages of Recovery

"The first ninety days of recovery are the most important for preventing relapse." According to statistics, approximately eighty percent of people have at least one relapse during recovery. Strategies to maintain sobriety are: be aware of triggers that may cause relapse; change previous patterns of self-defeating behaviors that led to drug use; Post-Acute Withdrawl Syndrome, PAWS, lasts for six months to two years after stopping drug use-- irritability, sleep problems, anxiety and depression are a part of the syndrome; do not participate in previous routines; form new and healthy relationships; maintain a structured and positive schedule; build a healthy lifestyle; maintain positive financial goals; confront past mistakes and work on learning from them so as not to repeat them; find a sense of balance in life; celebrate milestones that are reached, especially those of sobriety; learn how to be calm and not overreact or become overwhelmed to situations.

Self-care is an essential part of the fight against drug use.

Strategies that should be incorporated into a regular routine include: make time for yourself everyday; mindfulness meditation can be used to reduce stress, anxiety, and depression; yoga is a great way to increase well-being and reduce stress; exercise is another way to decrease stress; getting enough sleep is an important aspect of a person's well-being; creativity is positive in expressing feelings-- examples are drawing, writing, poetry, music, and dancing; having pets is a way to have unconditional love given to us; having a few special friends rather than a large number helps us round out life; outdoor activities help take us away from the hectic life we live; shut off cell phones for a few hours during the day; volunteering and being kind to other people gives us a good feeling.

PART SEVEN

The Role of Communities and Schools

"Change will not come if we wait for some other person, or if we wait for some other time. We are the ones we've been waiting for. We are the changes that we seek." Barack Obama

<u>Communities</u>

Throughout the years we have seen a shift in the role that communities play in the lives of its citizens. While women were once stay-at-home moms, that has changed with more women having careers and being in the workforce. Children find themselves being latch key kids, coming home to an empty house, and being on their own until parents arrive home from work. Neighbors are less apt to be able to support each other as had been the case many years before. The African proverb, "It takes a village to raise a child," has lost its place in our society.

As the drug epidemic in the United States continues to grow, we must find ways to help provide resources to our families. It is up to parents to advocate for changes within their community. We need after school programs to keep teens involved in healthy activities. Community leaders can join with schools, religious groups, and community agencies to provide recreation and sports. Businesses can be asked to develop programs offering teens jobs. Local government agencies can offer financial support for programs, perhaps by obtaining grants.

Along with these suggestions, advocates can reach out to local hospitals and talk to them about developing programs to help educate teenagers about the dangers of drugs, cigarettes, and alcohol. Counselors can be approached to work with teens to address emotional issues. As many families don't have mental health insurance, perhaps therapists can be spoken to about doing pro bono therapy.

Law enforcement agencies in many areas are involved in working with youth of all ages. For example, many cities have the Police Athletic League, in which officers coach sports, provide after school support, and other activities for the teens.

Encourage your community to get involved with National Prevention Week, a public education initiative that provides tools throughout the year to educate about the dangers of substance abuse.

"Involve communities in raising awareness of substance use and mental health issues and in implementing prevention strategies, and showcasing effectiveness of evidence-based prevention programs;

Foster partnerships and collaborations with federal agencies and national organizations dedicated to improving public health; and

Promote and disseminate quality substance abuse prevention and mental health promotion resources and publications." For more information visit: https://www.samhsa.gov/prevention-week/about (SAMHSA)

Finally, because of their addiction and history of legal problems, many of those who are in recovery have a difficult time finding a job. Sara told me how discouraging it was to send out applications and either never receive answers or be rejected time after time. She often talked about how being clean was harder than using drugs. It was heart-wrenching to hear those words—and probably for her to have to say them.

An important part of getting communities involved would be to have local businesses and local government agencies hire people who are in recovery. Education should be offered to those who want to go to college or trade school. Internships should be extended, with the possibility of a job upon completion. While we all need inspiration and for people to believe in us, a person in recovery is especially needy in this area. For them to believe in themselves, others must show that they have faith in them, too. For more information on how to provide help for jobs, read about the Supported Employment (SE) Program. https://www.samhsa.gov/criminal-juvenile-justice/grant-grantees/transforming-lives-through-supported-employment-program

<u>Schools</u>

Traditionally, schools had the responsibility of providing an education to children. The goal was, and continues to be, to prepare them for college or trade school. As society has changed, the schools have taken on new responsibilities. One of these is to educate students about the dangers of drugs and the impact addiction can have on their lives. As has been stated in an earlier section, it is important to recognize early behavior problems and put interventions in place at an early age.

So, how can parents get involved at the school level? As a parent your voice is the loudest and strongest one to be heard, for the simple fact that nobody loves your child as much as you do. I urge you to use that voice. Join the parent association at the school. Ask to see the curriculum that is in place for drug education and, if there isn't one, use your voice to start one. Start with the principal and go higher, if necessary.

As a school social worker, I worked closely with the guidance counselors at my schools. They not only worked with students on their academics but also on their emotional wellbeing. The counselor is a good resource for you to talk to about educating students about the dangers of drugs. They often facilitate educational groups and perhaps you can suggest that they run some about drug prevention. The counselor also can provide resources to parents.

Teenagers benefit from "seeing" and "hearing" rather than just being told. There are people in recovery from substance abuse and alcohol addiction that want to prevent others from taking the path that they did. Suggest to the school that they reach out and have assemblies with some of these people so that students can hear their story.

Working in high schools, I found that teenagers like to have someone at the school who takes an interest in them. Because schools are so big today, it is sometimes difficult for the staff to be able to act as a mentor. However, there are many mentoring programs that are available to the schools. If your school doesn't have one, speak to other parents and advocate for a program at your child's school. You'd be surprised how many retirees love to volunteer at the schools and provide inspiration to young people.

"According to the National Institute on Drug Abuse, children who struggle in school when they are between 7 and 9 are more likely to be using addictive substances when they reach 14 or 15." This would be essential information to discuss with school administration and guidance at the elementary level. The earlier that prevention programs are initiated, the greater the chance of stopping later drug use.

PART EIGHT

Advocate for Change

"Never doubt that a small group of thoughtful committed citizens can change the world. Indeed, it is the only thing that ever has." Margaret Mead

<u>Role of Government</u>

While it may be true that changes can be made by people joining together for a common cause, it is also true that one person can make a difference. The initiatives and laws that have been discussed in this book show that changes can be made. But there haven't been enough, and the drug epidemic has only become worse. To have laws passed, we must become active and contact our local, state, and federal representatives. The change may start with the citizens, but the officials have the power to put those changes into effect. Laws must not only be passed but must be enforced. As citizens and parents, we have the responsibility and the right to save our children. Contacting the politicians is just the first step. The next is to make sure the laws are enforced in our communities.

Get involved by joining groups that advocate for change. Start petitions and get your friends involved. Change takes time but the effort is worth it. If we don't stop the drug epidemic in our country, we will continue to lose our children.

PART NINE

Inspirational Words

<u>Inspirational Words</u>

The following was provided as an inspirational message for young people by someone who overcame her drug habit several years ago and cares about people. Please share with your child.

"To the old me:

If I could say anything to the old me, it would be that I wish that I had taken the time to ask you what was really bothering you; so maybe then you wouldn't have felt so alone, and the drugs would be your only escape. I wish I had let you know more often how much I appreciated and loved you for you, and that no matter how hard things got, that I would love you harder than your addiction.

So, the old me is gone and although it's taken much darkness to find my light, there's one thing I do remember telling the old me; "It's okay to ask for help!" "It's okay to not be okay!" and "It's okay to say we have a problem!" All it takes is one baby step into the opposite direction you've been taking, and the faith of a mustard seed to believe in yourself. To whomever may be reading this, I may or may not know you or your struggles, but you my friend are NOT alone. The world is beautiful and there's always someone there to listen. Just never forget that you're worth it!"
NGK

"Parents can help their children by being loving and strong. It starts with simple conversation. Young people need to be exposed over and over and over and over to the ramifications of drug abuse. They need to see pictures of meth users. They need people to go to the schools and talk to them. Parents, be nosy and trust your instincts. If you suspect your child is using drugs, have him tested. Be in the room when he takes the test. Better yet, take the child somewhere and have a professional test him. I have heard parents ask, 'What can you do when they are fifteen and sixteen years old?" My answer might be, 'Does your child live with you? If so, you have total control. Take away privileges, car keys, bedroom doors. Set boundaries and stick to them." Brenda Seals, author of "Son Down, Son Up."

Sometimes we can be inspired by people we come across in life to find the strength we need to make changes. The following is a story about Elton John taken from an article in a special edition of Time Magazine:

"Despite being nearly three decades clean, singer and pianist Elton John is still haunted by his drug -and alcohol-fueled past. 'I still dream, twice a week at least, that I've taken cocaine and I have it up my nose,' John told NPR in 2012. 'And it's very vivid and it's very upsetting, but at least it's a wake-up call.' Throughout the 1970s and '80s, the exuberant rock legend lived life through a drug-altered haze. The performer credits his sobriety to meeting Ryan White, a teenage hemophiliac who had contracted HIV through a contaminated blood transfusion. 'I had the luck to meet Ryan White and his family,' he said during a Harvard University talk in 2017. 'I wanted to help them, but they ended up helping me much more. Ryan is the spark that helped me to recover from my addictions and start the AIDS foundation. Within six months (of White's death), I became sober and clean, and have been for 27 years.'"

PART TEN

Conclusion

Writing this book was the most difficult project I have ever taken on and perhaps the most meaningful. My hope was to have it finished by the end of 2020, and then by February 28th, which was the one-year anniversary of Sara's death. I found myself spending more time staring at my computer than doing any writing. Learning about the different drugs and the horrors involved with their use was painful. Reading about the history of drug laws and current statistics made me angry—angry that things have only gotten worse in all of these years.

I learned a great deal about the impact drugs have on the brain and body of a substance abuser. I learned about risks for substance abuse, and I learned about early interventions to try to prevent the addictions. Many factors are involved in a child's life that may determine whether they will turn to drugs when they are older. I learned a lot and while I learned it, I wished I had known it thirty-five years ago.

It would have been easy to just put the book aside and tell myself that I'd finish it one of these days. But I want to help educate parents about the drugs and about behaviors that can lead to addiction. I want them to be aware that there are interventions to help change the behaviors at an early age, and resources that are available to families. By writing this book, I hope to save families from going through what my family has endured. I want to help prevent someone from taking that first drug.

When someone dies of an overdose, he or she becomes a statistic to the rest of the world. To the family of that "statistic," the loss is forever. Writing this book has not made Sara's loss easier to bear; but hopefully it will help prevent families from suffering a loss as great as mine. Perhaps it will help teach parents how to guide their children to make the right decisions; to begin communication with them at an early age and to build on it through the years; and to teach them how to choose positive friends.

Terms

Addiction: "Compulsive drug-seeking behavior where acquiring and using a drug becomes the most important activity in a user's life."

Barbiturate: depressants that control the nervous system. Results in sleep and sedation.

Benzos: major tranquilizers that cause sedation, muscle relaxation and sleep.

Cognitive Behavioral Therapy: clients are taught positive coping skills to deal with problems before they escalate.

Dependence: **Physical dependence** on drugs is the change that takes place in the body because of prolonged drug use. **Psychological dependence** is the user's perception of the need to have the drug.

Depressants: decreased alertness, attention span and energy due to lower heart rate, blood pressure and respiration rates. (Used to be referred to as "downers").

Detoxification: a medical process that treats the physical effects of with drawl.

Fentanyl: a potent synthetic drug that has been approved by the FDA to relieve pain. It is one hundred times more potent than morphine and fifty times more potent than heroin.

Gateway Theory of Drug Addiction: "Most people who use illegal addictive drugs first used drugs like alcohol, tobacco or marijuana." These drugs are said to be gateway drugs.

Heroin: processed from morphine (poppy plants) is a white or brown powder. Highly addictive, it presents a high risk for overdosing and may contain ingredients that the user is not aware of.

Intensive outpatient program: day treatment program for up to twenty hours a week for two months to one year.

Naloxone: a medication that quickly reverses an opioid overdose, restoring breathing. It is administered as an injection or nasal spray.

Narcotics: also known as opioids, are derived from opium.

Opioids: family of drugs derived from the poppy plant and used for pain management.

Outpatient treatment program: six to eight hours of therapy per week.

Overdose: caused by too much of a drug being taken at one time.

Psychoeducational groups: group therapy in which members are educated about drug use and taught coping skills.

Recovery: "A process of change through which individuals improve their health and wellness, live a self-directed life, and strive to reach their full potential." (SAMHSA)

Residential program: twenty-four hours a day for one month to one year.

Stimulants: reduce fatigue, produce a euphoric feeling, and stimulate a person's brain and body.

Resources

adolescenthealth.org
Ala-non
Alcoholics Anonymous
American Association of Poison Control Centers 800-222-1222
Center for Disease Control (cdc.org)
childmind.org
connectsafely.org
Crisis Text Line (741741)
dare.org
Drug Enforcement Administration (DEA)
drugabuse.gov
drugfree.org
drugfreeworld.org
Drugs of Abuse. A DEA Resource Guide (2020 and 2021 editions)
Family Resources Center
Federal Department of Agriculturef (da.gov)
hazeldenbettyford.org
Helpcenter.org (211 is a national telephone number that provides referrals for services in communities)
Journal of Youth Development (Model Youth Programs: A Key Strategy for Developing Community-University Partnerships Using a Community Youth Development Approach
kidshealth.org
Local Community Mental Health Centers
lung.org
Nar anon
Narcotics Anonymous
National Helpline (800-662-4357)
National Institute on Drug Abuse
nationalmentoringresourcecenter.org
parentactiondrugs.org
shatterproof.org
Substance Abuse and Mental Health Services Administration SAMHSA.org
Substance Abuse Service Hotline (844-804-7500)

talkitout.org
http://theaddictioneducationsociety.org
verywellmind.com

Books

1-2-3 Magic (Thomas W. Phelan, Ph.D.)

Addict in the Family: Stories of Loss, Hope, and Recovery (Beverly Conyers)

Addictive Thinking: Understanding Self-Deception (Abraham J. Twerski, MD)

Buzzed: The Straight Facts About the Most Used and Abused Drugs from Alcohol to Ecstasy. 5th Edition. (Cynthia Kuhn)

Hold On to Your Kids (Gordon Neufeld, Ph.D. and Gabor Mate, M.D.)

In the Realm of Hungry Ghosts: Close Encounters With Addiction (MD Gabor Mate)

Parenting Teens With Love & Logic (Foster Cline, MD and Jim Fay)

Self-Esteem for Teens (Lisa M. Schab, LCSW)

Sincerely, Addison's Sister (Jessica Akhrass)

Son Down, Son Up (Brenda Seals)

The Addiction Inoculation (Jessica Lahey)

The Science of Addiction (Time Magazine Special Edition)

The Self-Esteem Habit for Teens (Lisa M. Schab, LCSW)

When Your Adult Child Breaks Your Heart (Joel L. Young, MD)

References

1-2-3 Magic (Thomas W. Phelan, Ph.D.)
12step.com
ABC News (3/8/2016) ("Resources for Heroin and Opioid Addiction, Treatment and Support"
adai.uw.edu
Addict in the Family: Stories of Loss, Hope, and Recovery (Beverly Conyers)
addiction.surgeongeneral.gov
addictioneducationsociety.org
addictionsandrecovery.org
Addictive Thinking: Understanding Self-Deception (Abraham J. Twerski, MD)
Alvernia University (online.alvernia.edu)
American Academy of Addiction Psychiatry (AAAP.ORG)
American Academy of Child and Adolescent Psychiatry (AACAP.org)
American Academy of Family Physicians (AAFP.org)
Australian Government Department of Health
Better Health Channel (betterhealth.vic.gov)
biglifejournal.com
Buzzed: The Straight Facts About the Most Used and AbusedDrugs from Alcohol to Ecstasy. 5th Edition. (Cynthia Kuhn)

cbsnews.com (2/6/2020) "Gray Death"
Center for Disease Control (CDC)
Center for Parent and Teen Communication (9/4/2018)

centeronaddiction.org
Childmind Institute (childmind.org)
childtrends.org
CNN (8/10/2020)
dare.org
deamuseum.org
Drug Enforcement Administration (DEA)
drugabuse.gov
drugfree.org
drugfreeworld.org
drugpolicy.org
farcanada.org (Families for Addiction)
Florida State University (FSU.edu)
Forbes (8/10/2020) "Marijuana Use During Pregnancy Linked to Autism in children."
Frontline PBS
Harvard Health Publishing
hazeldenbettyford.org
Health Care Resources Centers (hcrcenters.com)
Health and Human Services (hhs.gov)
health.harvard.edu (1/1/2019)
history.com

Hold On to Your Kids (Gordon Neufeld, Ph.D. and Gabor Mate, M.D.)
huffingtonpost.com
Journal of Youth Development (Model Youth Programs: A Key Strategy for Developing   Community-University Partnerships Using a Community Youth Development Approach)
kidscreektherapy.com
kidshealth.org
Lung.org
Mayo Clinic
Medicalnewstoday.com
Merriam Webster Dictionary
NAADAC.org. (The Association for Addiction Professionals)
National Center for Biotechnology Information (NCBI)
National Conference of State Legislatures (NSCL)
National Institute on Drug Abuse (NIDA)
National Institutes of Health (NIH)
National Mentoring Resource Center (nationalmentoringresourcecenter.org)
ncbi.nim.nih.gov
New York Times
ojp.gov
Parenting Teens With Love & Logic (Foster Cline, MD and Jim Fay)
parenting.com
Partnership for Drug-Free Kids
positivechoices.org

positivepsychology.com/goal-setting
Promising Strategies to Reduce Substance Abuse (U.S. Department of Justice, Sept 2020)
psychologytoday.com
reference.com
Self-Esteem for Teens (Lisa M. Schab, LCSW)
Shatterproof.org
Singlecare.com
Son Down, Son Up (Brenda Seals)
stopbullying.gov
Substance Abuse and Mental Health Services Administration (SAMHSA)
talkitout.org
talkitoutnc.org
Teens, Drugs & Violence: A Special Report. Office of the National Control Policy (6/2007)
teensmartgoals.com
The Addiction Inoculation (Jessica Lahey)
The Jerusalem Post (7/18/2012)
The Science of Addiction (Time Magazine Special Edition)
The Self-Esteem Habit for Teens (Lisa M. Schab, LCSW)
U.S. Department of Justice
USNews.com (1/18/2021)
Verywellfamily.com

Verywellmind.com
weallrisetogether.org
When Your Adult Child Breaks Your Heart (Joel L. Young, MD)
wholefamilyapproach.org
youth.gov

Please follow the blog that complements this book for up-to-date information and resources:
https://herstarforevershines.wordpress.com/2020/03/15/example-post/

About the Author

Phyllis Babrove is a semi-retired Licensed Clinical Social Worker who has lived in Florida for over fifty years. After retiring as a school social worker in 2015, she took online writing courses and has had two short stories published, and has self-published four works of fiction. She has also written a series of articles for a social work magazine about non-traditional students. Phyllis likes to travel to New England with her husband.

Books by Phyllis Babrove

When Shadows Linger
Envelopes of Hope
My Name is Rebecca: A Novelette
The Primrose Garden

Made in the USA
Columbia, SC
16 May 2022